Paris

By Stéphanie Ledu
Translated by Sarah Moroz
Illustrations by Laurent Richard

MiLAN

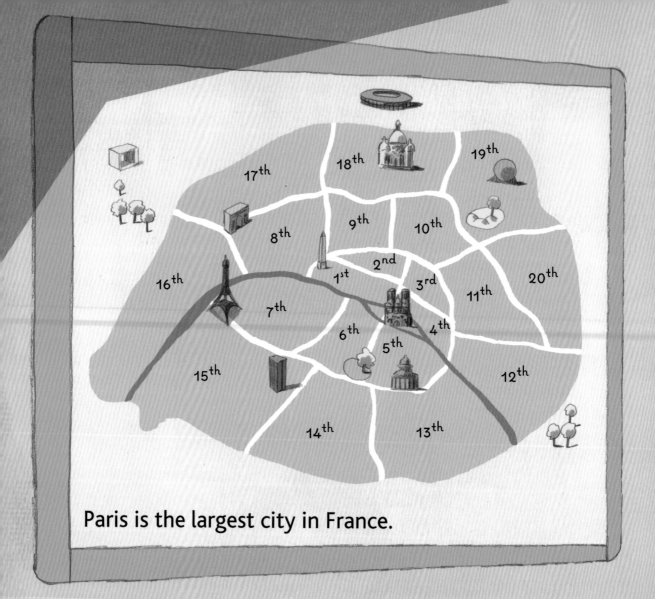

Paris is the largest city in France.

It is divided into 20 **arrondissements**, or **districts**.
On a map, they circle around like a big snail.
You can see the **Seine**, the river that flows through Paris.

4

Paris is the **capital** of **France**.
Big decisions are made at the **Élysée Palace**;
this is where the **president** lives.

The Élysée Palace

The Montparnasse neighborhood

The Sacré-Cœur

The Opéra Garnier

The Place de la Concorde

There are many other famous monuments in the city...

Very chic and always buzzing, Paris is the most-visited city in the world! Tourists love to people-watch on the **Champs-Élysées**. The avenue extends towards the **Arc de Triomphe**.

Click! Everyone takes a picture here, to be able to proudly say: "I was there!"

To get from one place to another, the **metro** is practical and speedy. You are never far from one of Paris's 380 **stations**.

But during the rush hours, when
Parisians come and go from work,
the metro cars are very crowded!

11

Direction: **Eiffel Tower**! Built in 1889
for the World Fair, it has become
the symbol of Paris itself...

You can get to the top level using the elevator.
You can get to the second level on foot,
if you are game to climb up the 704 steps.

How about a stroll alongside the water?
Each day, hundreds of tourists board boats
for a short ride on the Seine.

Here is the Pont-Neuf, which is
the oldest of Paris's 37 bridges!

The **Notre-Dame Cathedral** stands tall at the tip of the **Île de la Cité.**

Exhibitions, strolls, performances: here it's impossible to be bored! Let's go see the Mona Lisa! This famous painting is exhibited at the Louvre, the biggest museum in the world.

Prefer animals? Head
to the **Grande Galerie**
at the **Jardin des Plantes**!

And this funny-looking building? It's the **Pompidou Center**. The exterior is covered with air ducts, water pipes and electricity vents. A long escalator brings visitors all the way up top, to the **Museum of Modern Art**.

Street entertainers perform on the square in front of the museum.

Do your feet hurt? Are you tired of the noise and the crowds? You can relax in one of the city's 500 green spaces. Here are the **Luxembourg Gardens**, one of Paris's largest open spaces.

At the **Buttes-Chaumont Park**, a lake,
a waterfall, cliffs, tunnels and footbridges
are laid out like a scene from a painting.

21

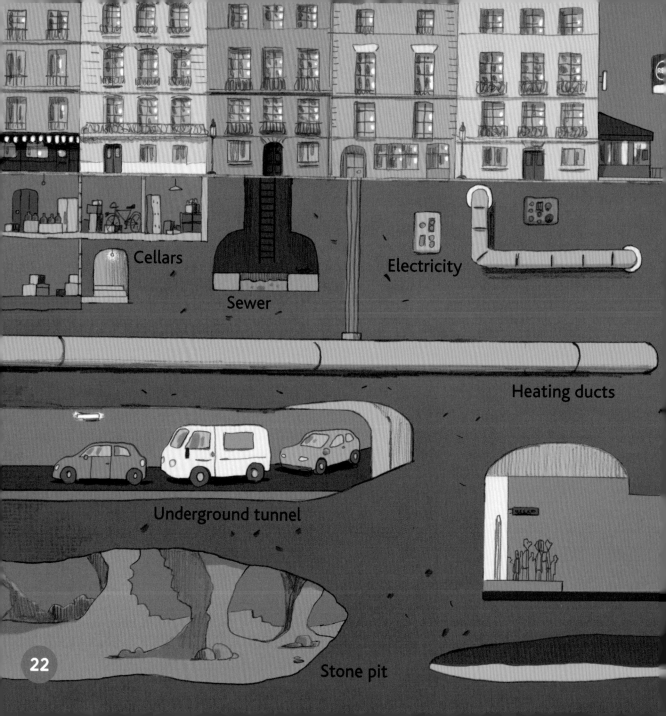

Cellars

Sewer

Electricity

Heating ducts

Underground tunnel

Stone pit

22

The city's **underground** has as many holes as Swiss cheese! Think of just how much is happening beneath your feet when you walk in the city streets...

Gas pipes

Mall

Metro

Parking lot

Groundwater

In Paris, traces of the past are everywhere.

Let's go to the **Arènes de Lutèce**: nearly 2000 years ago, the **Romans** watched gladiators fight here.
It's the city's oldest monument!

Let's wander through the lovely covered walkways, built 150 years ago. In those days, elegant Parisians would stroll here, sheltered from the rain...

25

Each neighborhood has its own atmosphere...

The **Buttes-aux-Cailles** in the 13th **arrondissement**, with its little houses, looks like a small village.

Here we are in Belleville, with its colorful outdoor markets. Parisians come from all over the world!

When night falls, the streets and the monuments of the capital are illuminated... High up on Notre-Dame, alongside the gargoyles of stone, you can watch the sunset... It's lovely, don't you think?

© Éditions Milan, 2011
1, rond-point du Général-Eisenhower, 31101 Toulouse Cedex 9, France

Droits de traduction et de reproduction réservés pour tous les pays.
Toute reproduction, même partielle, de cet ouvrage est interdite.
Une copie ou reproduction par quelque procédé que ce soit, photographie,
microfilm, bande magnétique, disque ou autre, constitue une contrefaçon passible
des peines prévues par la loi du 11 mars 1957 sur la protection du droit d'auteur.
Loi 49.956 du 16 juillet 1949 sur les publications destinées à la jeunesse.

Mise en pages : Graphicat
Relecture : Catherine McMillan
Dépôt légal : décembre 2011
ISBN : 978-2-7459-5547-0
Achevé d'imprimer au 2e trimestre 2019 en Roumanie par Canale
editionsmilan.com